Published by New Generation Publishing in 2021

Copyright © Susan Withers 2021

First Edition

The author asserts the moral right under the Copyright, Designs and Patents Act 1988 to be identified as the author of this work.

All Rights reserved. No part of this publication may be reproduced, stored in a retrieval system or transmitted, in any form or by any means without the prior consent of the author, nor be otherwise circulated in any form of binding or cover other than that which it is published and without a similar condition being imposed on the subsequent purchaser.

ISBN: 978-1-80369-074-2

www.newgeneration-publishing.com

New Generation Publishing

This book is dedicated to Alesia who we met perchance 5 years ago in Florida. We immediately became firm friends and have remained so.. Unfortunately COVID has interrupted our friendship but we are hoping it won't be too long before we can meet up again. After writing this poem for Alesia it was she who encouraged me to go to print and it was she who suggested I combined my new found love of poetry with my culinary favourites.

All the recipes I have chosen have a special significance and will offer ideas on how to make a basic recipe special, giving culinary tips designed to impress your friends and guests.

I have suffered from Parkinson's disease for the last 17 years and have raised over £5000 to support research into Parkinson's.
 A percentage of the proceeds from this book will go to them.

Poem for Alesia

Our first meeting - was it pure chance?
Or was it really meant to be?
Did God have a hand in our meeting?
Yes, I do believe in Destiny

We formed a bond
which cannot be broken
We understand each other
no words need be spoken

We have found new friends because of you
and had new experiences too.
We have enriched each others well-being
and our fun has lots of meaning

We miss each other's company
and hope to rendezvous soon
Doesn't matter where
Either UK, US or the moon!!!

Hope your Birthday was fun
Shame we could not be there
But when we reunite
We'll show you how much we care

> The recipe I have chosen is broccoli and cheese soup. Alesia is a great advocate for healthy eating and loves this home made soup.

Recipe Broccoli and cheese soup

Ingredients
2 broccoli stems cut into small pieces
100g cheese of your choice (grated)
1 onion chopped
1/2 pt chicken stock
1 potato chopped
knob butter
1/4pt milk

Method
In a large pan melt butter and add chopped onion and potato. Cover with a lid and cook for 3 - 4 mins till onion begins to take on colour
stir in broccoli and add stock
Bring to boil, place lid back on and simmer till potato and broccoli are soft (about 10 mins)
Add salt and pepper to taste
Remove from heat and, using a food processor, liquidise the soup
return soup to the pan and add cheese.
Add milk according to your preferred consistency. (Can be frozen)

Serve with crusty bread

One of my early poems was written after a visit to Chelsea flower show where my friend's son Graham won a silver gilt medal for his artisan garden. He designed a garden featuring a rusty old digger which had been transformed by nature into a thing of beauty. This inspired me to write the poem

poem The abandoned Quarry

The old abandoned Quarry lies still and calm
Where once the diggers would cast their arm
With strength and purpose, Now they lie useless,
Amongst the undulating ground, Where Nature has taken back control
And relaid a carpet all around. The diggers have now found A new purpose -
A structure to be admired -
To provide support -
To hold precious water -
Where nature and forgotten machinery, can live together in a new-found harmony

CHELSEA FLOWER SHOW 2019. The Artisan Garden

Graham's mum Elaine is my longest standing friend. Together with our partners we have travelled the world. She is always there to support me, particularly with my fundraising and she never lets me down.

We do lots of fundraising events to support research into Parkinsons and for the past 2 years we have cycled 26miles (a marathon) at a combined age of 138 years raising over £1500.

Poem For Elaine -

Together we've travelled far and wide
With our faithful partners at our side

Our first trips were skiing in the snow
Courcheval, Les Deux Alpes and Lake Taho

Cruising was then the name of the game -
Europe, New York, China
Cycling over The Golden Gate
There was nothing finer

Our road trips took us to Sri Lanka
And Yosemite National Park
Loving the giant trees, the elephants
And taking long walks till dark

Many times we've been to Chelsea
To see the flower show
Marvelling at the displays, the family accolades
And watching our friendship grow

My long term passion is fundraising
And you're always there to support
With prizes, plants and cycling -
A Marathon? Who would have thought?

Together we have done so much
And more is yet to come
Lets grab it while we can
And let's have lots more fun

A marathon for Parkinson's

> Of all the desserts, one of her favourite recipes is rice pudding, a dish which in her opinion is underrated. It can be made extra special by adding extra ingredients such as cream, sultanas, vanilla and /or nutmeg

Recipe Special Rice pudding

Ingredients
100g pudding rice
butter, for the dish
50g sugar
700ml milk
pinch of grated nutmeg or strip lemon zest

Method
Heat the oven to 150C/130C fan/gas 2. Wash and drain the rice. Butter a 850ml baking dish, then tip in the rice and sugar and stir through the milk. Sprinkle in the nutmeg and top with the lemon
Cook for 2 hrs or until the pudding wobbles ever so slightly when shaken

> You can make it look more impressive by serving in a stemmed glass and adding a fresh fig or other fruit for decoration

Elaine also has a lovely damson tree in her garden which is laden with damsons in autumn. I always collect these to make damson gin which is so simple to make and only has to be soaked for a week. However if you can stand to leave it longer the flavour becomes more intense.

After decanting the gin I use the gin soaked damsons to make chocolate liqueurs. Delicious!!!

Recipe Damson gin and chocolate liqueurs

Ingredients
300g damsons (washed)
150 g sugar
600ml gin

Method
Wash damsons then pat dry and place on a baking sheet
Place in freezer and leave for a few days for the skins to start to split
Place damsons in a kilner jar together with sugar and gin
The ingredients will probably fill more than one jar
Replace lid and shake vigorously to dissolve sugar
Place in a dark cupboard and leave for a week (or 2) if you're patient.
Keep turning and shaking the gin
You can see by the changing colour of the gin how effective it has been
Taste after a week or 2 to see if it is to your liking
If using more than one jar you can choose to open just one for starters
Decant into screw top bottles which have been sterilised and ENJOY

Chocolate liqueurs
Remove stones from the damsons which have been soaking in the gin. I do this by flattening them with a fork
Using a plastic mould, place the damsons(stones removed) in bottom of moulds

Melt a large block of chocolate and pour into moulds on top of damsons

allow to set then ENJOY!!!

> Michelle is my niece. She lives with her husband and two young children in Essex. She leads a busy life juggling work, childcare, out of hours classes and keeping fit, into her busy schedule. I just don't know how she manages. I am her Aunty and her nickname for me is AS (aunty Sue) This poem is dedicated to her.

A day in the life of Michelle

Hi AS cant talk for long
must take the kids to school
then I'm off to work
I'm not late as a rule

Hang on whats that noise?
Ollie,s lined up his cars
Jack has tripped over them
and knocked them near and far

Ryan - get a move on
Jacks due at football
If you don't get him there soon
He's going to miss it all

Must go soon
I'm off for a run
Got to keep my steps up
So tonight I can have a bun

Who's at the door?
its hello fresh again
Delivering our weekly shop
so I don't have to think
Or use my brain

Ryan - are you chef tonight?
to give me a break
Just pick any menu
and get it done for goodness sake

Off out with the girls tonight
For a few cocktails - wont get drunk -
But then again **I MIGHT**

> The recipe I have chosen is a quick and easy lamb and chickpea casserole as she is constantly looking for convenience whilst producing tasty healthy meals

Recipe Lamb and chickpea casserole

Ingredients for 4
400g lamb mince
2 onions chopped
2 carrots grated
2 garlic cloves grated or finely chopped
tin chickpeas
2tbs tomato paste
2 tbs harrissa pate
400ml chicken stock
2 ciabatta

Method
In large frying pan, brown the mince 4-5 mins and season with salt and pepper
Once cooked drain off excess fat and aadd onions and carrots
Cook until softened 3-4 mins
Once veg is soft add garlic, tomato puree and harrissa paste
Lower heat and cook 1 min
Add chicken stock
Drain and rinse chickpeas and add to lamb mixture.
Check seasoning simmer for 8-10 mins until mixture has thickened stirring occasionally
Serve with warm ciabatta

Lamb and chickpea casserole

I met my friend Dee at work and we have remained friends for the past 30 years. Dee thought that cooking and hosting a dinner party required a special skill, but after years of being a guest at my dinner parties she has realised that they can be as basic or elaborate as you wish to make them, and the most important ingredients are the friends you invite.

poem Dee, my special friend

I know I sometimes ask a lot
With my quizzes, games and what-not

But you're always there to play along
Even when I've lost the plot!!

Fun times we've shared
over the years
Much joy and laughter
-and a few tears

I hope this snapshot of things past
Will help to make your memories last

Poem what is a friend?

If you're not well they care
If you have bad news - they share
If you want a chat, they've time to spare
If you need a hand, they're always there
If you want some fun, they let down their hair

I know on you I can depend
Dee, my special friend

She particularly likes to make this dessert which is so quick and easy and can't fail. If served in Martini glasses it looks impressive

recipe Dee's impressive mango yogurt

serves 4
450g tub mango and passion fruit yogurt
2 ripe mangoes

Chop 1 mango into small pieces and place in bottom of Martini Glasses
Top up the glasses with the yogurt
Decorate with a sprig of mint
Puree the other mango and pour on top
Refrigerate until serving

Looks impressive, couldn't be easier

My friend Lesley, is a fun loving party girl who loves to travel. She started her working career helping her parents on their fruit market stall where she would yell out her wares - hence her nickname loud Lesley. She has recently acquired a cockapoo which has become the love of their lives, hence this poem.

poem To Lesley

Hello, my name is Lesley
Some would call me loud
You could hear me all over the market
My Dad was very proud

We love to go to Turkey
Where we have a little place
its great just to chill there
and take life at a slow pace

We love our little sports car,
We're in the Morgan Club
She takes us all over the world
And is programmed to end at a pub

Stuart, I'm so sorry
I'm in love with someone else
You'll have to take 3rd place now
or be left out on the shelf

Rosie's her name
She's cute and cuddly with long golden hair
She melts my heart
and I've no love left to spare

Don't worry says Stuart
I don't mind the BLAH
We'll all get together
For a **MENAGE A TROIS**

Rosie the heart-breaker

The dish I have chosen for Lesley is a chicken and chorizo risotto as she loves dining al fresco and this is a good alternative to bbq. It is a one pan meal and can be cooked outside on a gas ring or a bbq.

Recipe Chicken and chorizo risotto.

If cooking this al fresco I suggest you prep all the ingredients beforehand and put them on a tray to carry outside so you don't forget anything. then use a heavy based saucepan to cook it either on an outdoor gas ring or on the bbq Don't forget to take out your cooking implements and a dish for setting aside

Ingredients
2 tbsp Olive oil
1 Chorizo, chopped
1 Red pepper, finely sliced
1 Yellow pepper, finely sliced
2 Chicken breasts, chopped
2 Onions, finely chopped
3 Cups of Basmati rice / enough for 4 people1 and quarter pints vegetable or chicken stock
1/4 cup white wine (optional)
Handful frozen sweetcorn
Handful of frozen peas
Parmesan cheese
Knob of butter

Method

Fry the onion in a large pan, as they begin to soften add peppers.

When they are beginning to brown, remove onions and peppers and set aside.,

Fry chorizo for a few minutes to release flavours then add chicken and cook until golden brown and cooked through.

Place aside and keep warm.

Return onion and pepper mix to pan and add rice.

Fry for 2 minutes. Add wine if using and stir till evaporated. Gradually add the stock.

Once all liquid has been absorbed and rice is soft enough, Add Chorizo, cooked chicken, peppers and the sweetcorn and frozen peas.

Stir for a further 5 minutes or until heated through..

Add the Parmesan and knob of butter. Stir through and season to taste.

Decorate with lemon wedges

Take the pan to the table and place in centre so everyone can help themselves

Serve with crusty bread

Friend Joyce was always the life and soul of any party, throwing one at a moments notice. Sadly, she lost her husband some time ago which turned her life upside down. However, she is still a party girl at heart and never wants to leave. She loves a song and dance. We meet her at a little wine bar where we have a sharing platter and a glass of wine (or two) whilst putting the world to rights.

Poem For Joyce

Hi girls - we need a night together
Its been so long
Seems like forever

You know I love to sing and dance
But these days
I don't get the chance

Beatles, Stones and Donovan
I know the words
To every one

Before we go out
I like to dress - to impress
In my Sunday best

Need my nails done, and my hair
Pleased you can't see my underwear

I'm late now, I'm in a flap
Still need to put on my slap
Meeting you girls is the best
But after a night with you
I need a rest

Come on girls, just one more dance
I've told you Joyce
There's not a chance

But I haven't done my LULU act
We've seen it before
And that's a fact

12 already?, I hear it chime
Can't wait
Till we meet next time

I have chosen the sharing platter for this recipe suggestion as it is something that can be easily assembled if impromptu friends arrive or you want the girls round for a chat and they won't leave. It always goes down well with a drink (or two) and it tends to fuel the conversation

Recipe Sharing platter for impromptu get-togethers

Use a wooden bread board or similar and fill with flatbreads, crusty bread, crackers, hummus, pate, cheeses, indian nibbles, dipping oils, quiche, sausage rolls, parma ham etc
Keep a supply of these in your freezer and impress your friends with your hosting skills

I started playing golf at the tender age of 70 "something off my bucket list)" and have met two lovely ladies whom I play golf with. I have written a couple of golf poems for them depicting life on the golf course

Poem Life on the Golf Course

I met them on the golf course
nearly 2 years ago
And what with COVID and such
progress has been slow

Theres Jan - ex head
whose calm approach is to be admired
But when i tried to copy her
sadly it backfired

She joins the competition every week
and has improved no end
But alas, her attentions have now been diverted
by another little friend.

Her beautiful new granddaughter
is taking up her time
She takes her for walks and sleepovers
And life is just sublime

Annette - the non executive chair
Eager to improve, and learning the rules to the letter
Hubby Lee tries to give her tips
But she thinks she knows better

She brings us little golfing gifts - mainly golf balls
She has taught her dogs to find them
and retrieve them when she calls

Then there's me -
Fraught with appointments and injury
Hope I can get better soon
I think there's more chance
of me landing on the moon

But I'll continue to try along with my friends
and who knows where it will end?

Theres always the social events,
for these you need no recompense
You just turn up and have fun
And hope no one recognises you
-as the useless one|||

Poem Perils of the Golf Course

Perils of the golf course

Its the back 9 today
Hope my friends can come and play
10 is not my favourite tee
The grass is too long for me

onto 11 - WHACK -
looking down
My ball is nowhere
to be found!!

At 12 Must make sure
I avoid the stream
Wow -gone straight over it
What a dream!

Next shot - Oh no!
I've gone straight in the pond
Just wait till I get my dry clothes on

13 is not a problem
if you give the ball some clout
on 14 - you're in the stream again
If you don't watch out

At 15 -Annette does a pirouette
To avoid Jan's ball
Lucky were not in a comp, I say
That's all

16, I must try to hit the ball straight
were nearly there -WHOOPS
Watch out mate!!

17 is your best chance
of scoring a par
thats so long as you
don't hit it too far

Final hole - no 18, Fairly happy with how its been

Now lets go to our favourite hole NUMBER 19

The Recipe I have chosen is pan fried salmon with cous cous. I have chosen this recipe as its a nice light meal to enjoy after a round of golf

Ingredients
1 salmon filet per person
packet cous cous (lemon flavoured)
2 tablespoons chilli sauce
watercress

method
Pan fry the salmon skin side down until cooked (about 5 mins)
prepare cous cous per instructions
serve in a bowl - place cuos cous first, sit salmon on top, drizzle chilli sauce over salmon and top with watercress

> Our family are waterski enthusiasts. It is a sport we can all be involved in together and we now have great pleasure watching our grandson oscar aspire to be a waterski champion. I wrote this poem for him following his achievements in a competition as I felt it was more personal than a card

Poem Oscar the waterskier

He started young - yes only two
His parents hopes were grand
The newspaper reported him as
Youngest skier in the land

He has carried on in leaps and bounds
Some say he has a skill
At 13 he's not far off the best
And his boots are hard to fill

With a quest for perfection
He is determined to train
To be a skiing athlete
Come sun, wind or rain

As each week passes
He skis without remorse
Trying again and again
To beat his performance on the slalom course

He is now at competition level
Where he's aimed to be for years
Showing grandad how it should be done
And beating all his peers

We wish you well Oscar
In all that you do
And hope the number 1 slot
Is soon in sight of you

Lots of love and best wishes

Grandma and Grandad xxx

The recipe I have chosen for him is Comfort pie and grandmas chips. My comfort pie is basically a cottage pie packed with a variety of vegetables which Oscsr doesn't realise he is eating.

Grandma's chips are made by chipping the potatoes, patting dry and placing on a baking tray. Sprinkle with cooking oil, salt and Parmesan if desired. Bake in oven 200 deg for about 20 mins.

From a young age oscar called these grandmas chips. He loves them

Recipe Comfort pie and Grandma's chips

ingredients (for4)
400g beef mince
1 onion chopped
1 carrot chopped
3 sticks celery chopped
small courgette thinly sliced
handful mushrooms sliced
chopped peppers(optional)
handful peas
Beef stock
passata
dash worcester sauce
mashed potatoes

method
fry mince in a little oil for 5 mins.
When browned add onion, carrot, celery, courgette and mushrooms.
Cook for 5 mins till soft
Add beef stock, worcesteer sauce and passata and simmer for 5-10 mins till mixture thickens
Place in oven proof dish and top with mashed potatoes
Top with grated cheese and bake in oven for 30 mins at 380deg

For a more unusual topping try using Cheese sauce instead of grated cheese then pop it under the grill

OSCAR WITHERS AGE 13 years

My husband Chris and I have been married for 40 years and I believe that our recipe for a successful marriage is our love of the same things ie holidays, music, food and friends. We love entertaining and I will find any excuse to have friends round. No celebration day ever goes unmarked.

Until COVID struck, I cannot remember a time when we did not have a St Valentines Day celebration. I always invite friends, prepare themed food and we end up with a quiz.

Poem

My Love

I'd walk a million miles for you
I'd even swim the sea.
I'd put you first every time
And never think of me.
I'd give you my last meal
And clean the car for free

I'd help you in the garden
I'd massage your sore back
I'd go wherever you wanted
All the way there and back

I'd love you for always
And do things happily
All these things I'd do for you
And I know you would for me

All my love Sue xx

The recipe I have chosen is La coeur de la boeuf bourguignon as it is one of my husband's favourites. it is very rich so he only has it on occasions. Perhaps that's why he likes it so much.

For an intimate suggestion for dessert, melt some chocolate in a pot and dip strawberries into it. You give one to your partner and he serves one to you - very sensual

Ingredients
1.6kg/3lb 8oz good-quality braising steak
4–5 tbsp <u>sunflower oil</u>
200g/7oz smoked bacon lardons or smoked streaky bacon, cut into 2cm/¾in pieces
1 large onion, finely chopped
2 garlic cloves, crushed
75cl bottle red wine
2 tbsp <u>tomato purée</u>
1 <u>beef stock</u> cube
2 large bay leaves
3 sprigs fresh thyme
25g/1oz butter
450g/1lb pearl onions
300g/10½oz chestnut mushrooms, wiped and halved or quartered if large
2 heaped tbsp cornflour
2 tbsp cold water
salt and pepper
chopped fresh parsley, to garnish

method

Trim the braising steak and cut into chunks, season with salt and pepper

Fry beef in 2 tablespoons of oil over a medium heat until nicely browned

Add a little more oil to the frying pan and fry bacon until brown and crispy

Remove bacon and fry off chopped onion and garlic for 5 mins till soft

Add bacon, onion, garlic to beef and pour over wine

Stir in tomato puree and water

Crumble in stock cubes and herbs and bring to simmer.

Transfer beef to ovenproof casserole and place in preheated oven 170C

Cook for 1 1/2 hours or until meat is very tender

Remove casserole, stir in the cornflour mixture followed by button onions and mushrooms

Return to oven and cook for further 45mins until the sauce is thick

To serve, remove thyme stalks and sprinkle over chopped parsley

Valentines Dinner Party

> Of course, I cannot miss out my beautiful granddaughter Sienna whom I adore. She is now 21 but I wrote this poem for her when she was 17. 4 years later, the words would be just the same

You have taken away all our fears
And emerged from Princess to Beauty Queen in 17 years

Some of your friends try to be
Like some kind of Celebrity

But you are the one who is unique
Your individual style is what you seek

You are way above the race
And set the others a good pace

We hope your future is a success
And your life is filled with happiness

Lots of love Grandma and Grandad

I have chosen a vegetarian dish for Sienna as she eats very little meat. When she was at University, every term beginning iI would make huge batches of meals and freeze them for her to take back to uni. She really appreciated this as it saved her time and money, Each meal I packed was sent with love.

TIP Money is very tight for students so if you can send them back with cheap to produce ready made meals then you are ensuring they eat healthily and you are helping to preserve their limited funds

Ingredients

Vegetarian Spaghetti carbonara (for 1)

! sm onion chopped
1 sm red pepper chopped
6 mushrooms chopped
1 garlic clove crushed
150ml single cream
50 g grated cheese

Fry onion and pepper till soft (about 5 mins)
Add mushrooms and garlic and cook for a further 3 mins
Stir in single cream and grated cheese and warm through

serve on top of a bed of spaghetti, accompanied with Garlic bread

> **Finally, I have written a poem for a very special person whom I would love to meet. If you know them, please let me know.**

poem for a very special person.

Got up this morning feeling pushed
too much to do, I'm in a rush
Before going to work hubby reminded me
that tonight we're having a dinner party.

Need to pick up his clean suit.
cook a meal and set the table
Need to take baby to aunty Mable

My hair's a mess and nails need doing
I feel just like a proper ruin
What can I wear? my clothes don't fit
I've put on pounds - maybe 5 or 6

Tonight is special
I need to impress
Please help me
I'm in such a mess

Don't worry says her friend, don't fuss
lets start with the meal - Octopus?
While its cooking we'll do hair and nails
'cause with this dish you cannot fail

I bought a new dress last week
On you it will look a treat.
You can wear it tonight, it makes you look slim
then next week we'll start going to the gym

Now phone Mable and ask
 if she can pick baby up at quarter past
and on her way pick up the suit
 and a bottle of gin - what a hoot!!

Now you're all ready with time to spare
Have a lovely evening and remember,
I'm always there

Can you name this special person?

I'm sure It's someone we'd all love to know, and for the lucky ones you already do.

I hope you enjoy my collection of poems. Most of them have been written in the past year. Prior to that it had never entered my head to put pen to paper in this way.

I hope you enjoy the recipes too, if you do, please feel free to pass them on to your friends with my love

Sue